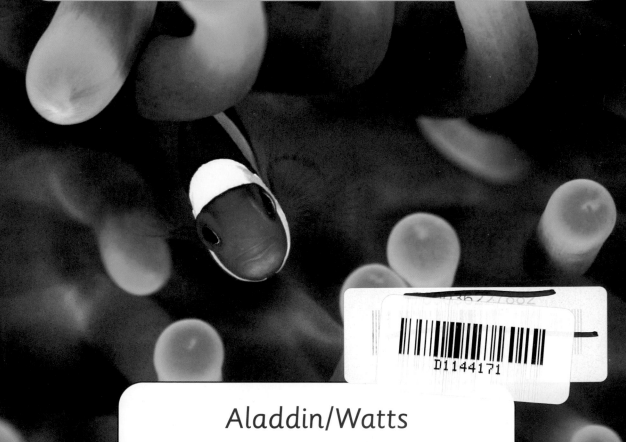

Read and Play
Sea Animals

by Jim Pipe

Aladdin/Watts
London · Sydney

sea

2

Here is the **sea**.

What lives in the **sea**?

3

fish

Fish live in the sea.

4

Fish
can swim.

5

crab

A **crab** lives in the sea.

A **crab** has claws.

7

turtle

8

A **turtle** lives in the sea.

A **turtle** has a shell.

9

seagull

A **seagull** is
a sea bird.

10

penguin

Penguins are birds. They swim.

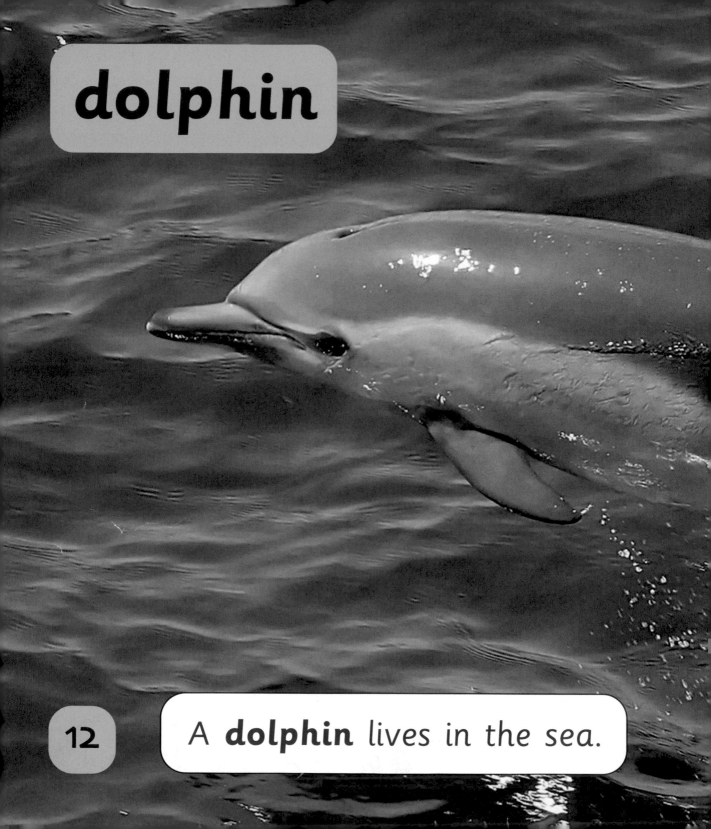

dolphin

12

A **dolphin** lives in the sea.

A **dolphin** jumps!

shark

14

A **shark** lives in the sea.

A **shark** has big teeth.

15

whale

16

A **whale** lives in the sea.

A **whale** is enormous.

octopus

An **octopus** lives in the sea.

seal

Seals live in the sea.

19

Who am I?

turtle

crab

shark

dolphin

20

Match the words and pictures.

How many?

Can you count an octopus' legs?

21

What am I like?

cow

jelly

horse

star

What do these sea animals look like?

Index

Can you find these pictures of sea animals in the book?

For Parents and Teachers

Questions you could ask:

p. 2 What lives in the sea? Ask children to think about animals that live by the sea (e.g. birds), in the water (e.g. seals, fish, sharks, jellyfish) and at the bottom (e.g. crabs, lobsters, shrimps, starfish).

p. 4 What colours are fish? Fish can be bright colours, e.g. reds, yellows and blues. Other fish are brown to help them hide in the sand.

p. 6 What can you see on the seashore? Ask children to think what they might see at low tide, e.g. crabs, seaweed, shells, sea birds.

p. 8 What other animals have a shell? Crabs, lobsters, shellfish etc. Explain that a shell protects a sea animal's soft body, like a snail's shell.

p. 11 How is a penguin different to other birds? Most birds can fly. Some birds can run fast, e.g. ostrich. But a penguin is built for swimming.

p. 14 What do you think a shark likes to eat? A shark's sharp teeth help it catch fish, squid and seals. Some sharks crush and eat shellfish.

p. 16 How long is a whale? Get a long rope (e.g. 10 m long). Get the children to unwind it – 3 lengths (30 m) is the same length as a Blue Whale.

p. 20 If they need a clue, children can look at the cover and back at pages 6, 8, and 14.

Activities you could do:

• Put several plastic sea animals under a sheet and ask the children in turn to "dive under the sea" and retrieve one of the animals. They can then tell the others about the animal they've caught.

• Cut a variety of seashell shapes in different shapes, colours and sizes. Ask children to sort / match them by colour, size etc. You could also describe animals that live in shells, e.g. mussels.

• Role play: Put children in groups of four and ask them to make an octopus with eight waving legs!

• Game: Have one child as the shark who must tag/catch the others, who are fish.

• Visit an aquarium to see real sea animals.

Paperback Edition 2009
© Aladdin Books Ltd 2007
All rights reserved

Designed and produced by
Aladdin Books Ltd
PO Box 53987
London SW15 2SF

First published in 2007
by Franklin Watts
338 Euston Road
London NW1 3BH

Franklin Watts Australia
Level 17/207 Kent Street
Sydney NSW 2000

Franklin Watts is a division of Hachette Children's Books, an Hachette Livre UK company.
www.hachettelivre.co.uk

ISBN 978 0 7496 8980 3

A catalogue record for this book is available from the British Library.

Dewey Classification: 591.77

Printed in Malaysia

Series consultant
Zoe Stillwell is an experienced Early Years teacher currently teaching at Pewley Down Infant School, Guildford.

Photocredits:
l-left, r-right, b-bottom, t-top, c-centre, m-middle
All photos from istockphoto.com except: 11, 22br, 23bl — Corbis.